Ode To Coffee

Written and Illustrated
By   Nina Tabares (Mayani)

English Edited By Amber Tabares West

Spanish Edited By Isis Tabares

Al CAFÉ

Ode to Coffee is inspired by coffee's impact around the world. It is a simple way of giving praise for its role in helping provide economic growth and stability to people of various cultures around the world for well over 500 years and counting.

TXu 2-926-392

ISBN-13: 978-1545091203
ISBN-10:154509120X

Printed by Create Space. An amazon.com company. Available from Amazon.com and other retail outlets, other online stores, other bookstores, and their distributors.
 Published in the United States of America

To My Mom who showed me

full of joy

the first white dot.

Para mi mama' que me mostro'

llena de alegria

la primera puntica Blanca.

A gentle breeze was moving the branches of the bushes at the tropical plantation.

Un viento suave movía
las ramas de las plantas
en la plantación tropical.

It was moving slowly.

as if rocking

a newborn baby.

*L*as movía
despacio,
como se le mece
la cuna a un bebé.

Looking closer at the bright green branches, there were tiny white dots.

Mirando cerca sobre
los tallos de las ramas verdes
se veían asomar unas
punticas blancas.

After a few days, the tiny dots became tiny white flowers.

Después de varios días las
punticas blancas
se volvieron flores pequeñitas.

A fter a thunderstorm, the sun

shone brightly. The next day,

little green bulbs emerged

beneath the flowers.

Pasaron varios días y después
de una tormenta el sol comenzó a brillar,
y al siguiente día comenzaron
a salir **pequeños bulbos verdes**
debajo de las flores.

The bulbs grew and grew.

feeling happy to be rocked by

the winds gentle movement.

Estos crecían y crecían

y se sentían felices de ser

arrullados

por el viento.

The sun continued to shine.

Finally,
the green bulbs grew
to their full-size fruit
of just half an inch.

El sol brillaba día tras día

haciendo crecer con su calor
los bulbos verdes que ya eran
de un centímetro de tamaño.

$\mathcal{T}$he fruit turned from green

to yellow while looking happy

at the great **sunshine.**

Las frutas cambiaron de color verde

a color **amarillo** mientras

miraban felices a la luz del sol.

Then they turned orange,

only a **short rain**

refreshed their skin.

Luego cambiaron de anaranjado.

Solo lluvias cortas

refrescaban su piel.

There was no rain

or wind for days

the warm sunshine dried the skin

of the emerging coffee beans,

changing the color from

orange to deep red.

*N*o había lluvia, no hacía viento.

El sol brillante tostaba la piel
de los granos nuevos del café,
que cambiaron de color
anaranjado a *rojo obscuro.*

There were the ones observing it

who came to take them away

picking only the mature fruit,

and making sure to leave the green beans

because of their bitter taste.

*L*os que lo observaban **vinieron**
a llevárselo
    recogiendo solo los granos maduros,
dejando los verdes
        por su sabor amargo.

Their cycle was finished

from white dots

to a brown earth color,

Su *ciclo estaba completo;*

de punticas blancas a color marrón,

.... and to fill up the air

with their **unique** aroma.

.........y a llenar a su paso

el aire de su *especial aroma.*

Nina Tabares was born in South America. After traveling with her husband in the military she fell in love with the beautiful State of Wa, that is now her home.

She has been painting oils for over 40 years and lately doing illustrations for her books.

Ode to Coffee is her 4th book and the second about Coffee. Her third Coffee book "Coffeesitos" will be published on 2017.

This books have been published by CreateSpace and Amazon.com. You can find them also in Ingram, Barnes & Noble, Nascorp.